Adam, Where Are You?

Restoring man back to his position

JARROD DUNN

Adam, Where Are You?

ACKNOWLEDGEMENT

I remember reading a quote one day that said "Many people are anxious about changing their present situation but unfortunately many of them are unwilling to do anything about it". This quote has been instrumental in the writing of this book. If there has ever been a time for men to arise it is now. Our generation is experiencing some turbulent times. We have seen some changes in our nation, society, and communities like never before. Among our homes, talk shows, and magazines we have individuals who are telling others how they ought to live. I'm convinced that if we can put the right piece of the puzzle in place we can begin to see things slowly but surely change. I believe the right piece of the puzzle is the man. The man holds the key to turning our nation, society, and communities around.

I want to thank my beautiful wife, Nichole, and my children, Jae'la, Aniyah, and Alex for the support, patience, and accountability they provide for me while I pursue the many projects that are connected to my purpose.

Adam, Where Are You?

I would also like to thank my Kingdom Restoration Center partners who believe in me and keep me motivated by your love, support, and dedication

Alexis Willis (Lady Lex), my editor for this project, thank you for the time you dedicated to help me get this message out.

Contents

Introduction

Introduction

When I began writing this book, I was incarcerated in federal prison. I can recall the day as if it were yesterday. I remember sitting in my room one morning thinking about my life and all the decisions I had made that had led me up to that point in my life. As I sat back in the chair of my desk inside my cell, I began to look at the pictures I had of my family posted on a board.

I looked at my beautiful wife and thought about how she was rearing a family by herself without my help. I looked at my children and thought how they were living a life without a positive male influence. The thought of me being incarcerated and not being able to provide any type of support was almost overwhelming to me because I knew my situation was not the predetermined purpose for my life. I couldn't help but to think about the countless number of men who were incarcerated physically and mentally. They lacked examples and role models and weren't able to receive the essentials needed to rear a healthy family.

Adam, Where Are You?

"I had to do something," I thought to myself, but what?

It was at this time that I began to take my pencil and yellow notebook and start writing "Adam, Where Are You?" During my time of incarceration I had come into contact with many frustrating days and disturbing nights. There were times I regretted the many years I had wasted here on Earth because I too was like Adam: naked, ashamed, and hiding myself from the presence of God.

I had begun living an immoral lifestyle at the age of 13. I involved myself with any- and everything, looking for something to give me purpose.

In 2004 I was indicted by the United States government. Immediately after my indictment I entered into marriage with a beautiful young lady who was the mother of my two daughters and one son on the way. I entered into marriage without a clue on how to be a leader, husband, and father.

Being the leader of my house was confusing, and trying to be a father was tedious, and on top of that my marriage was out of order.

Adam, Where Are You?

Parenting was rough, my lifestyle was uncertain, and, piling on, the federal judge sentenced me to 145 months (12 years) in prison on my first offense.

I know, first hand, what it is like to be haunted by the question in the eyes of my children and the voice of my Eve: "Where are you?"

I've came into contact with a man whose child was gunned down because of a bad drug deal, and while he was sharing the story with me, I could feel the mother speaking within herself: "Adam, where are you?"

I've witnessed young women grow up in the community and reach adolescence, a point in their lives where they had to make important decisions, but because of a lack of guidance from their fathers, they made bad choices, leaving them in remorse and asking the question, "Adam, where are you?"

I've been in churches and witnessed the confused look on the pastors' faces as they viewed their congregations of women and wondered within themselves, "Adam, where are you?"

Adam, Where Are You?

I've been motivated to write this book by my experiences and in hope that it will help many Adams to take their God-given positions and reclaim what rightfully belongs to them.

I trust that this book will prick your conscience and challenge your spirit to move towards the destiny God intended for you since the beginning.

My challenge in this book is to motivate you to consider your spiritual, physical, and emotional position in the various aspects of your life.

Every man needs to understand his position, where he is in his relationships to his family and friends.

He also needs to know what his purpose is in life and inside his community.

This book will help you understand your purpose as a man. It will inspire you to start dreaming again. It will also motivate you to be an effective leader and persistent in your community involvement.

"Adam, where are you" in your relationship, position, family, church, and community?

Chapter 1

Foundation

Foundational scriptures
Psalms 11:3; Genesis 1:26;
Genesis 2:7; Genesis 2:21-27

I have had more conversations with men pertaining to their relationship with God than I can count. Oftentimes, the focal point of the conversations would shift from them to the women of the family. They make statements like, "My wife is a God- fearing woman" or "My grandmother is very religious" and last "My mother attends church every Sunday."

They exalt the matriarchs of the family and assume that just because the women are active inside the church it gives them the pass with God.

Adam, Where Are You?

Perhaps men feel they will have to give up their leisure time to develop the same strong relationship with God they see many women obtain. Maybe they view God as an elective- something that you can choose to have or not.

Although a relationship with God is a choice, many men pass the baton to their wives, ushering them and the children out the door every Sunday while they go play sports, drink, hang out with friends and cheer their favorite sports team on. I even heard a pastor joke that most men have their religion in their wives' name.

If we are going to be effective in leading our homes, we must first realize that we, men, are the foundation on which the home is built. The man is the foundation to building sacred homes, stable families, and strong communities. Myles Monroe states that a lack of understanding in the roles men play will have us continually seeing women who suffer from abuse by angry men, children who wrestle with resentment, and society bearing the scars of deterioration.

Adam, Where Are You?

Do you know why? Because an ill-informed man is a dangerous man.

Foundation is important. If the foundation is destroyed, what can the righteous do, as David asks in Psalms 11. In Hebrew, foundation means basis, moral support, and purpose. When God began to build humanity, He began like any other builder by laying the basis, moral support, and purpose.

In Genesis 2:7, after God formed Man, He blew into his nostrils the breath of life and Man became a living soul, after God created him, God placed Man in the garden, Eden, to dress and keep it. He then gave Man a vision (which will be discussed later) before he brought Woman into the picture so that Man could be effective in what He called him to do.

Genesis 2:21-25 gives us the story of how Woman was created and presented to Man. God brought her to Man and created the first family. Family is the foundation for society and man is the foundation for the family. If we are to fix the crisis of unstable families, weak society, and homes lacking the importance of being sacred, then we must start with the foundation- the man.

I like to use the analogy of a house to give you an example of the life of a successful man and to demonstrate the characteristics of a strong foundation. There are four vital characteristics of a good foundation:

- Strong
- Solid
- Deep
- Stable

The foundation is the most important element of building a house. Every builder knows how imperative it is to lay a strong, solid foundation. Without it, the integrity of the house is compromised. The same is true for men. If a man builds his foundation on anything other than Christ, then he will find cracks and fault in the sub-structure of his life and he will be living on shaky grounds. The foundation must be laid properly if the house is to stand properly.

I mentioned previously that in order for us to fix society we must fix the family. In order to fix the family we must address the condition of the man and get him back into position connected with the right foundation, Christ. For man to be successful, he must be established on Jesus Christ, the bedrock of truth.

Adam, Where Are You?

Points to Ponder

- Man is the foundation to building sacred homes, stable families, and strong societies.
- The success or failure of a man is determined by the strength of his foundation.
- Man must be connected to the right foundation.

Chapter 2

Position

Foundational Scriptures
Genesis 2:4-5

I don't know how time slipped by me. My thoughts raced as I rushed out of my apartment. I knew I had to meet with my mentor at a certain time and I did not want to be late. After running to reach the destination, I climbed the stairs slowing my pace in fear that my mentor would not be there. I entered his room and I found him sitting at his desk with all the prepared materials for our meeting.

I sat down. *Whew, I made it!* The moment I sat down, he arose from his chair, closed his books, gathered the prepared materials, and said, smiling, "I'll see you next week."

Adam, Where Are You?

I was stunned. "Are you serious?"

"Yes. Suppose I had one million dollars to give you and asked you to meet me at a certain time and place. Now suppose you were late. The one who is going to bless you isn't obligated to wait on the one who is supposed to receive it. The blessing had a condition and it was the place and time. You were not in the right place at the right time so you were out of position missing a blessing for that day. See you next week." I looked at him with complete understanding. I was out of position.

Where are you positioned? Keep in mind that I am not asking you to identify your physical location. I am asking, are you in your proper position taking care of your responsibility?

It is an uncomfortable but necessary question. Some men do not like to talk about this touchy issue because it causes self-examination.

We do not have a problem talking about cars, jobs, sports, women, and a variety of other things, but when we come face to face with the reality of our position, we shut down and try to avoid the uncomfortable issues.

Adam, Where Are You?

I had to evaluate my position several times throughout my life. I had no clue where I was nor did I have any direction relying on clichés like, "God knows my heart" did not get me the answers I needed to get into position.

Genesis 2:4-5 explains that God created the heavens and the earth, every plant and herb in the field before it grew but He had not caused it to rain because there was no man to till the ground. This text is interesting because it says that God did not allow anything to grow for the simple fact that there was not a man in position to till the ground.

When a man is not in position, he hinders the growth of everything that he is connected to. I believe with all my heart that this is what our society is experiencing. We are seeing families and communities being restricted from reaching its full potential due to men being out of position. This has been evident in my life before.

When I recall the earlier years of my life, I am reminded of how my wife reared three children alone. She was the one who imparted wisdom and values into our children. Her dreams and aspirations were put on hold because she had to tend to overwhelming issues in the family. I had to face reality and realize that I was a hindrance to my family because I was out of position and in turn my environment was feeling the effects of my poor decision making.

Position vs. Location

I quoted previously that when I ask you about your position I'm not speaking of your present location. In Genesis 3:9 God asked Adam a perplexing question, "Adam Where Art Thou?" God wasn't asking Adam where he was physically because He already knew. The question that God proposed to him was nothing more than opportunity for Adam to accept responsibility for being out of position.

I know where I am at present because there are many indictors that tell me of my present location. My position has everything to do with my responsibilities. Here are a few questions that you can ask yourself to determine whether you are in position. 1. Are your actions irresponsible? 2. Does your decision tend to be selfish? 3. Are you determined to make sure that you and your needs are taken care of before anyone else?

Today I can say that my family is benefiting from me taking ownership of my position and they are reaping the benefits of productivity.

My wife owns a number of profitable businesses and is a mentor and leader inside our community.

My children are leaders in school, sports, and ministry, and I truly believe that none of this would be possible unless I stood face to face with the hard truth that I was out of position.

Don't get me wrong- my family was able to survive but I believe I prevented them from thriving.

Adam, Where Are You?

Can you honestly say you are allowing all that belongs to you to prosper simply because you are in your proper position?

Points to Ponder

- Position will determine whether something functions properly.
- Opportunities will always pass by someone who is out of position.
- Being out of position hinders the growth of everything a man is connected to.

Chapter 3

Vision

Foundational Scripture

2 Corinthians 4:18; 2 Corinthians 5:7

Proverbs 29:18; Jeremiah 29:11

The atmosphere was charged with anticipation. It was the first time I would get to see my family without looking at them through a television monitor. Escorted by the court marshals, I noticed my family waiting on me with smiles on their faces that said everything would be OK. My attorney motioned for me to stand next to him as the preparation for sentencing began. In those quick moments, I began to think about my older brother who had been sentenced to life in prison a month earlier; and of my twin brother who, just a few days before, received several years for a conspiracy conviction. This was a pattern.

Adam, Where Are You?

"United States of America versus Jarrod Dunn..." echoed through the courtroom and captured my attention. The judge informed the courtroom why we were there, what my charges were, and asked if I had any final remarks. Not knowing how to respond, I lowered my head, raised it quickly and said, "God has the final say-so."

Furious with my response, the judge expressed his disdain for me and labeled me a menace to society. "One hundred and forty-five months," he said slamming down his gavel.

I was stunned. As I looked around the courtroom, I did not know what to think but I remember the confused look on my wife's face. I turned to look at my Mom and then my Dad who reassured me that everything would be Ok. That was the last time I would ever see him.

It was a long walk back to the holding cell and an even longer day. All I could think about was the many years that I would spend in prison for a first-time offense. I wrestled with all the negative voices that had spoken into my life. I replayed what the judge said and could hear the people who said I would never amount to anything. The thoughts were so real because all I could see was that my situation lined up with what had been spoken.

Just as I could not see past my current condition, many men cannot see beyond their own circumstances because they have no vision. He is either functioning without a purpose or has accepted what has been spoken over his life by family, authority figures, or friends. As a result, we can find more men mimicking sports figures, music artists, gang leaders, drug dealers, and charismatic speakers rather than Christ. A lack of vision will always cause a man to wander but having a clear vision for his life will allow him to stay focused and be the man he is called to be.

Consistently I have come into contact with men who live their lives based on sight and not vision. There is a difference: sight shows you the way things are and puts emphasis on your current circumstance; yet vision shows you what shall be *in spite of* the current situation.

Adam, Where Are You?

In 2 Corinthians 4:18, Paul encourages the Corinthian church members to fix their eyes not on what is seen but on the unseen since what is seen is only temporary.

He continues to encourage them to walk by faith and not by sight in 2 Corinthians 5:7. It is a natural instinct for a man to be moved by sight because it is one of the five senses: sight, touch, smell, taste, and hearing. These senses can have us moving into a direction that is not connected to our destiny.

Use your senses to your advantage and create awareness about your situation rather than make rash decisions that will leave a lasting negative impact.

Vision will allow you to keep your senses in alignment with your goals and remain productive.

Adam, Where Are You?

Proverbs 29:18 tells us that if vision is absent then the people will perish. In this context, the word vision means "revelation". The God's Word translation says "Without prophetic vision people run wild."

Another way to define vision is your purpose in pictures. Although we will cover purpose in Chapter 5, understand that having vision will give you the capacity to see further than your eyes can look. Vision is the greatest source of hope and is important because it allows you to see beyond natural limitations, reveals the potential inside you, and is your road map to your destiny.

A life with vision keeps a man focused and intentional but unfortunately a large number of men lack direction and therefore we are seeing families suffering, health dissolving, and questionable spirituality; this has left a devastating impact within our homes and communities because where the man goes everyone else follows.

Adam, Where Are You?

In the book of Judges, we learn the story of Samson and it is a great illustration as to why vision is important. Judges 16:21 says, "But the Philistines took him and *put out his eyes*." Samson, the mighty man of God, had reached a point in his life where time had run out. Samson's character flaws had taken him to a place where what used to work to his benefit no longer did. He was taken captive by his enemy, the Philistines, and was brought into bondage. The first thing his enemy did was put out his eyes.

Any time you stop someone from seeing, you immobilize him. When you immobilize him you hinder him from receiving the blessing from the Lord. Without his eyes, Samson was no longer able to move forward. What we see is very vital. Whatever has your vision has the ability to control your destiny.

It is important to be decisive and to choose a life of vision so that you will know the direction you must take. I can remember when I had to make a decision to live my life with vision instead of sight. It was during a dark period when everything around me looked dismal and unpromising. Motivated by the scripture in Jeremiah 29:11, which says that God has a plan for me and thoughts of peace and not evil to give me an expected end, I realized I did not have to accept the circumstances that were right in front of me. Inspired to a make change, I put forth effort to pursue goals and aspirations to live out the destiny that God had for my life and I encourage you to do the same.

Are you living your life based on what has been spoken over you or have you blocked yourself from your greatness because your present condition doesn't tell you that it is possible? My man, your current situation is not permanent. I want to encourage you just as Paul did the Corinthian church and tell you that you can get in right standing with God, live the life that you envision, and walk out the purpose and destiny God has for your life.

I made the decision to live with vision and not sight so that I can live and not die. This decision allows me to have a better marriage and helps my children to know me as a man with vision rather than someone living with the limits society and others had spoken over my life.

Points to Ponder

Sight	Vision
Emphasis on your current situation	Shows you what shall be
Magnifies the things that are seen	Allows you to bypass your natural limitations
Focuses on the five senses	Your purpose in pictures
Enemy of vision	Source of hope

Call to action

Are you viewing your current situations and circumstances with sight or vision?

If you are viewing your situations with sight, take the model on the previous page and write on a blank sheet of paper what you see with sight and what you expect to see with vision.

Chapter 4

Family

Foundational Scriptures

Psalm 133:-1-2; Corinthians 2:11; John 4:24;
Genesis 12:3; Mark 3:25; Malachi 4:5-6;
Ephesians 1:3; Romans 12:1-2; Mark 9:23;
Romans 10:17; Joel 2:25; Psalms 55:22;
Matthew 6:33; 2 Thessalonians 3:13; Galatians 6:9

I loved Sundays because of weekly family gatherings. As a child, my mother would take me and my siblings to my grandfather's house and my cousins and I would play backyard football, walk the neighborhood, and listen to family members tell jokes and stories about times past. The day was always full of anticipation because we were very close, woven together by the examples of the matriarchs of the family. We laughed, cried, and celebrated one another over years of gatherings

30

each week. Growing up with this example, I would always say that I wanted the same example and deep sense of unity in my family.

Motivational speaker Les Brown said, "Life is a fight for territory and if you're not willing to fight for what you want, then what you don't want will eventually creep in."

Men have to fight like never before for their families. It is amazing how the family structure has dissolved from previous generations and has left families without a clear understanding of how a unified family functions.

Let's define family. According to Strong's Concordance, the Hebrew word is "mishpachah," which means "circle of relatives, class of persons, a tribe of people."

Webster defines it as a group of individuals living under one roof and usually under one head, a household.

From the two definitions we see that a family is cohesive unit.

Adam, Where Are You?

I like the wording Webster uses because it calls a family a group. A group is two or more individuals having a unifying relationship.

A family was something God created for the sole purpose of functioning together. Psalm 133:1 reminds us it is good and pleasant to dwell together in unity, emphasizing the importance of unison and how it is beneficial.

Today we see many families separating, leaving children in this generation with tainted views on the function of a true family.

This unclear perception has children joining gangs, destructive organizations, and cults just to find structure so they can feel secure.

God had originally arranged the family to be a healthy social structure whereby individuals learn how they ought to function within the boundaries of their homes. When that social structure isn't intact, it can have individuals within that environment yearning for some type of order. A lack of order inside the home and family can have a young boy confessing that he is with the red or the blue or have young women confused about their sexuality. Many of the gangs, clubs, and organizations promise us the very things we look for within our home-structure.

Unity is a vital component to a family because you can live in the house with someone and be involved in daily activities with them but still be separated from them. There may be some reading this book saying, "I'm not separated from my family. We all live together in the same household and do things together."

You don't have to be out of the house to be separated from your family. Remember, Psalms says it is pleasant for brethren to dwell together *in unity*. What about the parent who has not told the child "I love you" or express to him how special he is?

As a child I very rarely heard my father say that he loved me. I knew that he did by what he did for us. There were times, though, I needed to hear the words and so I dealt with many unnecessary emotions.

Adam, Where Are You?

Most men find it hard to express their emotions because we are brought up in a society that teaches us men are supposed to be strong and tough, which is mistranslated as unemotional.

A man's emotional love for his family can reinforce emotional stability in the family unit.

God is so wonderful that He did not want us to be in suspense as to what a family should look like and how it should function. Family is one of God's holy institutions. Family was instituted to represent Him. Not only did God establish the family on Earth, He also spoke blessings over it so that it could function according to the purpose for which it has been created. He created the natural institution of family as a reflection of the spiritual representation of family. Family is holy in the eyes of God and He has chosen family to represent Him and His relationship to the Body of Christ.

Where there is unity, the blessings of God are always in operation. God has blessed the family but there is an attack to try to separate it because a house divided against itself cannot stand. The enemy has launched an onslaught against the family to keep family members separated, and to bring them back together it requires the men to step up and say, "I am ready to restore my family."

As I mentioned before, the man is the foundation on which the family is built. I'm convinced that in these last days God will release the spirit of Elijah upon the men of this generation and that they will have a heart to see families restored and repaired (Malachi 4:5-6).

All it takes is that one man stands up and represents his family. Will you be that man? Will you be the man that God has called you to be?

Restoring Families

There are many barriers men must overcome. If we are going to start the process of reconstructing our families, the most important barrier needing to be eradicated is that of negative thinking. Paul explains the importance of this in Romans 12:1-2. He tells us that our minds need to be transformed by renewing it. If you are reading this book and you have the mind- frame that you cannot change your family structure, then the first thing you must do is renew your mind with the word of God. You must build faith by the word of God. Everything that we need in order for us to be successful men has already been given to us. Ephesians 1:3 tells us that we have already been blessed in the heavenly places with whatever spiritual gift that is needed.

I know many of us might have families that look as if they are out of reach. Some of us might even have family members who had been so dysfunctional for so many years that we might not want to deal with them. I come to give you good news *that all things are possible to him that believeth* (Mark 9:23, KJV). We have a right to have a blessed family. As an example, the blessing God placed on the family can be traced all the way back to Abraham. In Genesis 12, God told Abraham that all the families of earth shall be blessed.

God is very interested in restoring our families but the restoration process begins with us. Remember what I said earlier, that one of the reasons God created a family was so it could represent Him and His relationship to His children here on Earth. The question we should be pondering isn't "Can my family be restored?"

I believe the question should be "Will I believe God for the restoration of my family?"

God promises us in His Word in the book of Joel that He will restore the years that have been wasted. (Joel 2:25). God promises us that He will give back unto us the years we missed with our family. Every year spent in separation, He *promised to give it back*. Every year that was spent in chaos and confusion, He *promised to give it back*. Every year that was spent in grief and lamentation, He *promised to give it back*.

Isn't it wonderful to know that God desires to restore the very things that we have lost? The things that are so dear to us, God desires to give it back.

It's important to note that just because God desires it doesn't mean we will have it. God's love is unconditional but some promises are conditional. Our faith is what positions us to start the process of restoration in our lives. If you have this desire to restore your family, I would encourage you to do what the scripture says in Mathew 6:33 seek the kingdom of God and His way of doing things. Because God knows the avenue we should take in order to reach our destination, when we seek God in the process we can work smarter and not harder.

My second suggestion is that you make yourself available to your family. The lack of availability can be common among men. Many men are interested in making a living instead of having a life. Bringing home the bacon is not the only means of providing for a family. We have substituted giving of ourselves for material things but one of the greatest gifts we can give our family is us.

Often times we don't realize how valuable we are in the eyes of others. This revelation came to me one day while I was meditating on the expensive gifts I had given my wife. I remember asking her about a pair of diamond earrings that I bought for her. She told me that she had lost them and I thought *wow, how could she mishandle something so valuable?* The more I thought about it, the more I realized, *why would she place a value on something I really never had an opportunity to see her wear?* I wasn't available to my family.

My last piece of advice on how to restore your family is to encourage you to be consistent. Second Thessalonians 3:13 says, "And as for you, brethren, do not become weary or lose heart in doing right but continue in well-doing without weakening (Amplified Version)." Often times we are tempted to get tired and lose hope as we pursue a desire that looks as if it doesn't want to come together. I want to instill confidence in you with words from Galatians 6:9 which says, "And let us not be weary in well doing: for in due season we shall reap, if we *faint not* (emphasis added)". If we continue in spite of the difficulties we may encounter, we will be rewarded because consistency is the key that allows us to see results.

Points to ponder

- God instituted family for the purpose of functioning together.
- You don't have to be out of the house to be separated from your family.
- The earthly family is to represent the example of the heavenly model.
- One of the greatest gifts we can give our family is ourselves.
- God is interested in restoring families.

Call to action

Name at least three steps you can take to begin the process of restoring your family.

Chapter 5

Purpose

Foundational Scriptures
Genesis 2:4-7; John 4:7

After preaching a message at the New Life Bible College in its soup kitchen, I stayed a little later than usual because I wanted to check on some of the families I had developed a relationship with. While I was standing around talking to one of the men, I noticed a young guy looking at me. After a few minutes passed he approached me and asked if I had any extra shoes that he could wear. I didn't have any on me that day but I promised I would meet him later in the week so that I could help him with whatever he needed.

I returned my attention to the other man and continued to encourage him. Curious about the young gentleman that inquired about the shoes, I wanted to get some more information about his situation. He began to tell me about his life and how things have been a challenge for him since he was 17 years old. A few minutes into the conversation he said something that made me think about so many other men. He said, "My wife and I walk back and forth to this place every day to eat and I'm tired because it seems like we don't have any purpose."

I thought *WOW*, because this is an unfortunate example of the aimless routine of so many men-just doing the same thing every day without intention.

The Importance of Purpose

Dr. Myles Monroe said, "When purpose isn't known abuse is inevitable." In essence, he was saying, When you don't know your purpose, you will develop the tendency to abuse yourself and others. Abuse comes from two words: abnormal use. When you don't know your purpose, you will abnormally use yourself for something other than what you have been created for. I often think about this statement because it shed so much light on issues I have struggled with in the past.

When you don't know your purpose, your ability to make good decisions is altered because of a lack of understanding your original design.

Let me give you an example. As I write this book, I am sitting in an office chair. If this chair could speak, it would be singing a sweet melody for the simple fact that it is being used according to its original design. Original design is an intentional blueprint for the purpose of the creation. The purpose for this chair is for me to sit in and not stand on. Standing on the chair would violate the original intention for which it was created. In the same way the chair was created with a purpose, you were also created with a purpose that aligns with your original design.

I've spent so many hours thinking about the choices I have made that were purposeless. I've severed good relationships, destroyed companions, misused and abused people, all because I didn't understand purpose. A woman or a young lady is being abused right now because some man doesn't know her purpose. A child could be receiving inadequate guidance from an authority figure who doesn't understand the child's purpose.

Purpose is defined as the reason something exists. God never created anything and then decided what it shall be later. He was intentional in His creation of us and He created us with a purpose mind. Genesis 2:5-7 tells us God had every plant and tree on the Earth but He wouldn't allow the rain to cause it to grow because "there wasn't a man to till the ground."

In verse 7, He formed Adam from the dust of the ground and breathed life into him. God created Adam for the purpose of managing the garden. The reason for Adam's existence in the beginning was for the purpose of carrying out his assignment on Earth.

Regardless of your present condition, you still have purpose. Your past failures and mistakes do not cancel out your purpose. Your present misfortune does not negate the fact that you have purpose.

Adam, Where Are You?

Purpose is the reason for creation. While you are reading this book, it is important that you know without question that you have purpose.

Man is made of three components: past, potential, and purpose. Let's explore all three.

Past

Past is what you have been through. Our past is interesting because people have a tendency to define themselves by their past. Many men are defining themselves by something they have been through or experienced. It's frustrating to see 50-year-old men still living their lives as they were when they were 20. Even Muhammad Ali, one of the greatest boxers of all time, discouraged this type of behavior and said, "If you still live your life at 50 like you did when you were 20, you have just wasted 30 years of your life."

So remember your past isn't the real you nor does it define you.

Potential

Potential is untapped power waiting to be accessed. The word derives from the root word "potent," which means power. Potential will wait to see a demand on it before it is released. If you have the capacity to accomplish a task in your own ability, then your potential will lie dormant. In other words, you maximize your potential when you step out of your comfort zone and stretch beyond your natural abilities.

I have tapped into my potential by sitting down to pen this book. I did not know a book was in me but when I began to think about the impact I wanted to have on men, I had to release my potential that was lying dormant inside me.

There is something inside every man who is reading this book waiting to be revealed.

Potential is the real you that no one knows. Your peers may be comfortable with who you are now but your potential will allow them to meet someone new who will have the ability to inspire them to maximize their potential too.

I've been around men who were full of gifts and talents but never tapped into that power. God has placed potential inside you and the way He is going to do the great in you is through what comes out of you.

Purpose

We have already discussed the importance of purpose at the beginning of the chapter but remember that purpose is the real you. God will always deal with His creation based on its purpose. When a man knows his purpose it can help him not to succumb to his current struggles. A purpose truly embedded in the heart of men can benefit his decision making because his choice will not be influenced by *where* he is but by *who* he is.

I want to encourage you to realize that your purpose is more important than your past. Maybe you don't know your purpose and would like some type of insight into figuring it out. I can help you. Follow the directions on the purpose discovery worksheet that is provided on the next page.

Adam, Where Are You?

Purpose Discovery

Discovering yourself to achieve your purpose and unlock your potential

1. What do you see in society that burdens or grieves you?
   Write down something you see around you that makes you either really angry or really sad. If you tolerate it, then it will not cause you to do anything about it. It is when you can no longer accept it that you are prompted to do something about it.

2. What groups of people are you passionate about (Circle one)?
    Circle only one group. If you find yourself wanting to impact more than one group then circle "people in general."

People in General	Children	Couples
Professionals	Adults	Teens
Families	Religious group	An ethnic group
Women	Singles	Non-Christians
Seniors	Men	Others
Singles family's households		

3. What should be your message to this group?
    Everyone has a message. Limit your words but think about if you were standing in front of the group you identified in question #2, what would you say to this group? Write it down.

4. Choose words as to how you would like to help the above group.(Circle Two)

Words are powerful. Take your time to choose TWO that will describe the impact that you want to have on the group you identified in question #2.

Motivate	Create	Discover	Encourage
Comfort	Lead	Empower	Influence
Impact	Nurture	Impart	Repair
Challenge	Equip	Minister	Serve
Change	revive	Develop	Organize
Renew	Other		

5. What do you want this above group to become as a result of your influence (Circle one)?

After having come into contact with you, what do you imagine this group will look like once you have impacted them with your message?

Examples:

To live a successful life

To be productive

Maximize their potential

To enjoy their life

To obtain more out of their goal

Others

6. Take the answers to the questions and follow the purpose
    code 4,2,3,5,

(Write the answer that you had for each number)

Write the answers to questions number 4,2,3, and 5 next to the
corresponding numbers below to form the Purpose Code.

4:

2:

3:

5:

Take the answers that you had for 4,2,3,5 and form a complete sentence with them. Try to minimize your words.

Example:

To equip and develop leaders to walk with purpose so that they may live a fulfilled life.

Write YOUR purpose below:

_____

_____

Points to ponder

- When purpose isn't known abuse is inevitable.
- A lack of purpose will alter your ability to make good decisions.
- Purpose is the reason something exists.
- Past failures and present mishaps don't cancel out your purpose.
- When you lack purpose, your life is an experimental project.
- Purpose can help you not to surrender to your current struggles.

Call to action

Take the answer from your purpose discovery and put it in a location where you can recite it and look at it daily.

Chapter 6

Role

Foundational Scripture

Genesis 1:27-28, Matthew 12:33, 1 Samuel 17:58, 2 Corinthians 5:10, Psalms 115:12, Proverbs 4:23, Romans 10:10, Deuteronomy 7:13, John 16:7, Romans 6:16, 1 Corinthians 9:27, 2 Corinthians 13:5, Hebrew13:8,

---

While taking my kids to school one morning, I received a phone call from a good friend and after catching up just before we ended the call he told me a story. His wife had called him when she was having car trouble. He picked her up, switched cars, and parked it in a sales lot for a couple of days until he could get a plan of action. Recently, he said, he had looked up the Blue Book value on the car and it was a low amount. A week had passed and after taking his wife to work, he realized that he

Adam, Where Are You?

still had the car parked in this same location. He pulled into the lot, spoke to a car salesman, and asked about a BMW for sale. The salesman assured him they could run the numbers to see if he could qualify for the vehicle. He ended up trading in the original car and driving off the lot with a car his wife wanted. After he told me the story I asked him how he felt. He said he felt so good because it really solidified his role as a man and husband.

Men are facing difficult times and are confused by the direction our society has taken. Growing numbers of women have taken dominant positions in what used to be identified as male's roles. It is not unusual to see women doing things that would have been considered unacceptable 20 years ago but now are acceptable. For example, in some instances we find the women instead of the men being the bread-winners, rearing the children, and providing for the household. Because women have had to shoulder the responsibility of the household, it has become common to see a woman display her independence before a man with an attitude that says, "I've done it all by myself."

Adam, Where Are You?

It looks as though the man's role is dwindling in our fast-paced culture along with changing values and norms. What role do men have in a culture where roles shift gradually? How do we define true manhood in a society that exalts women and puts men down? Let's investigate where men should turn in order for them to have a clear understanding on the role of a man. Keep in mind that, although people, cultures, and societies change, God doesn't. It is very important we realize that, although things in our society have changed, the plan and purpose for mankind is still the same as it was from the beginning.

In order for us to get an understanding of how something is supposed to operate, we must start with its original design and how did it functioned in its infant stage. For us to figure man's original design, we first must go back to Adam. Genesis 1:27-28 says, "So God created man in his own image, in the image of God created he him; *male and female* created he them. And God blessed them, and God said unto them, *be fruitful and multiply, and replenish the earth, and subdue it*: and have dominion… (emphasis added)."

Adam, Where Are You?

In the beginning, God gave man everything he needed. Verse 28 reveals to us the first thing God did for mankind: He blessed us. Blessed is "Barak" in the Hebrew which means to kneel, bless abundantly, altogether, greatly. God provided everything Adam needed and with this provision came a responsibility.

Now let's explore the five aspects of the role God has given to mankind. Please keep in mind that God gave the mandate to *humanity* but in this section I will relate it to the role of the man.

Fruitful

The first command God gave after He had blessed mankind was to be fruitful. Fruitful means to bear fruit, bring forth fruit, to make grow, and increase. If I take the definition of fruitful into consideration, it would probably read something like this "and God blessed them, and God said unto them, *bear* fruit, bring forth fruit, make grow, increase." In essence, God said to Adam, "be productive." "Productive" means "producing or able to produce large amounts of goods, crops, or other commodities."

It amazes me how I was taught that this verse meant God wanted man to produce as many babies as he could. This interpretation is sad because we do have a generation of fatherless children but this is not the true intent of this scripture. In the context of Genesis 1:26, being fruitful is not just limited to producing children; it is also a mandate to be productive.

One of the roles of a man should be that he produces.

What is fruit? The word "fruit" in the Greek means "as plucked." Fruit is a representation of the product that the tree produces. When you see a married woman, she is not always identified by her own identity, but often is known by whom she represents and that is her husband and family. She is the product of this tree.

I love the analogy the Bible gives talking about fruit in Matthew 12:33: "either make the tree good, and his fruit good; or else make the tree corrupt, and his fruit corrupt; *for a tree is known by its* fruit (emphasis added)."

In this passage, Jesus clearly states that a tree is known by the fruit it produces. It's not hard for a person to define which tree is an apple or orange tree because of the fruit hanging from the tree.

The apple doesn't fall far from the tree

Let's take a look at another powerful example of how the fruit is a reflection of the tree by examining the story of David and Goliath. In 1Samuel 17, David, a little shepherd boy, was about to conquer one of Israel's biggest adversaries. He was asked by his father to go and check on his brothers who were fighting a battle. When David noticed that the army of God was stricken with fear, he stepped up, slew Goliath, and gave the children of Israel a victory. After the battle something interesting occurred. David's victory caught the attention of King Saul who wanted to know who David's father was. His success on the battlefield spoke volumes about the tree he came from.   After the battle was won and the celebration was in progress, a simple question arises: Young man, who produced you?

As I reflect on my life, I realize I haven't always produced good fruit. Don't get me wrong: I was still producing but what I was producing was not sweet and enjoyable instead it was sour and bitter. It's almost embarrassing to think about how I would allow others to see the product of my fruit -immorality, uncleanness, unfaithfulness, and inconsistency- not realizing that this was what I was producing and what I was known by.

Many men today aren't being productive. They aren't realizing that the very things they are producing are reflecting them. If the fruit is good or bad it still represents what has produced it. The tree is known by its fruit!

Do you realize that others know you by what you are and have produced? What type of fruit are you allowing others to pick from your tree?

Multiply

God also told Adam to multiply. Multiply means "to make many or manifold; increase the number, quantity."

God not only told Adam to bring forth fruit, He also commanded that he take what he has produced and multiply it. God requires that what we produce should increase.

The relationship we have with our wife and children should increase. Our business, knowledge, and activities should all increase.

Contrary to the mandate to multiply is the tendency to be complacent. Complacent means, "contented to a fault, self-satisfied and unconcerned."

I often wrestle with the fact that so many men are living a life of mediocrity.

I can remember a point of my life were I have said *I'm all right. I'm satisfied right where I am* but I had become complacent. There was a time in my life when I had this mis-conception that God wanted me just to be happy and satisfied with what I had and where I was in life. It was very frustrating because I had no one to run to for instruction because my elders and peers had been brought up under this same doctrine. They would say such things as "you have to be content with what you have" and "This is the will of God for you" and "God is in control."

Challenge yourself to be around people who aren't comfortable with living an ordinary life.

I was talking to a man one day who told me that he made his mind up to soar with the eagle rather than hang with the chicken. The difference, he explained, is that eagles soar but chickens barely fly.

The people who were around me were chickens, barely flying, and satisfied with a mediocre life. Initially, I accepted what they said but there was a conflict inside me. I knew there was more.

How to Multiply

In order for us to begin this multiplication process we must first have an understanding of a few things. First, we must know our purpose. Purpose is vital because if a man does not know his purpose then he is aimlessly walking. The man who doesn't know his purpose is going nowhere because he is aiming for nothing. We mentioned in the last chapter that purpose is the reason for which something exists or is done, made, or used.

Revisit your purpose statement from the last chapter because it is vital and it is the first step to start the journey to multiplying. You have to find a way that you can take what God has given you and multiply it into the lives of people. If God has blessed you to teach, you can take that effective teaching and put it into the lives of others so they may influence others. That is multiplication.

Take Jesus' relationship with the disciples as an example. Jesus understood the principle of multiplication. Multiplication is depositing something of value on the inside of others so they can receive an increase or harvest on what has already been given to them. By depositing the Holy Spirit on the inside of the disciples, He could now be in multiple locations at one time and in return he could receive a greater harvest. *Multiplication's main concern is not self but others.*

If God has blessed you to cook, can you figure out a way to package your product and put it on the market so that it can benefit others besides your family? Whatever you talent may be can you find a way to distribute it to other so that they may profit?

Fill

Another job that God gave man was to *replenish*. The word replenish means "to fill or add to." God told Adam to fill or add to whatever is needed on Earth. In essence, God said to Adam, "I have given you everything you need and if you don't have it add it and make sure it is filled." Wow! This is awesome. God has placed every resource inside man so that if something is not there he has the ability to add to it.

Adam, Where Are You?

In order for us to operate on this level, we must first be operating effectively with the two primary principles that God has given us, to be fruitful and multiply. If these two principles are operating in our lives, then we will have enough means to take from one place and *add* to another. So wherever I'm needed and if it lines up with my purpose, then I have the ability to meet that need. It also means that if there is a void in the lives of others I have the capability to meet the need.

When a business opportunity comes my way, I have sufficiency to meet that need. If I'm in an environment that is lacking structure, because I'm blessed, I can add to it so I can fill the place with the blessing of the Lord.

If I'm an educator that means I'm supposed to *add* to and *fill* others with the knowledge that is needed to help them make the right decision. If I'm in the arts and entertainment field, I'm to *add* and *fill* others with the joy and comfort that is obtained through the partaking of my gift.

Maybe you are in the medical field; that is a wonderful place to *add* and *fill* others with hope.

Whatever area of expertise you are in, it is your job to *add* and *fill* others with your God-given gift and talent.

God has called us to take what we have and *add* it to our children, wives, and community. Wherever we are, we are to *add* unto and *fill* that place with all that God has given us.

Subdue and have Dominion

This word "subdue" is very interesting. Subdue means "to conquer and bring into subjection."

When God gave Adam his mandate, we see that He also gave him a great responsibility. God told Adam, "Now that you are doing all that I have created you to do, take control of it, manage it, and make sure that it flows properly."

This is an amazing revelation and lets us know that if something is out of control then it is not being subdued. If my life, business, family or health is not flowing the way that it should be, then I'm not subduing it.

Make an observation of your surroundings, take note of what may be out of control, and bring it into subjection.

After God had finished giving Adam his mandate, He told him to have dominion. Dominion means to influence all that belongs to you by ruling and reigning. The root word of dominion is "domain" which is an area of territory owned or controlled by a ruler or government. Much like kings have domains, we are to have dominion over all that has been entrusted to us.

Points to ponder

- Although things in our society have changed, the plan and purpose for mankind is still the same.
- People, cultures, and societies change-God doesn't.
- One of the roles of man is to produce.
- Challenge yourself to be around people who aren't comfortable with living an ordinary life.
- Multiplication's main concern is not self but others.
- God has given us the ability to create.

Call to action

How have you defined your role as a man?

Has the way you defined your role lined up with the way God defines the male role? If not, how can you redefine it?

Chapter 7

Mentor

Foundational Scriptures

Acts 8:30-31

I wanted to add this section in the book because I really believe that mentoring is very vital for men. I'll talk more about this topic and go into greater depth in my upcoming book "Where Is Jethro?" I can truly say that where I'm at right now in my life had a great deal to do with the men who have been instrumental to me

To give an example of how important mentorship is let's take a look at the story of Philip and the Ethiopian in Acts Chapter 8. On his travels to Gaza, Philip met an Ethiopian of great status who came to Jerusalem to worship reading the Book of Isaiah. Prompted by the Holy Spirit to go near the chariot, Philip approached him, heard him reading, and asked him, "Do you understand what you are reading?"

Adam, Where Are You?

In verse 31, the Ethiopian responds, *"How can I except some man guide me (emphasis added)?"*

This passage has spoken volumes to me regarding mentorship. There are so many men who are by themselves trying to navigate through life but they are ineffective because of a lack of guidance from other men.

I will never forget when I started this journey and made my mind up to do God's will. I had four key mentors who helped shape who I am today. They took me under their wings to show me who I was in Christ, how to stand strong in the Lord-relying on His ability and not my own-and that I didn't have to be like any other man, but should just be myself.

All these men played a major role in my life in helping equip me to be a teacher of the Good News.

I also learned the importance of being a man of character who lives a life of excellence.

Adam, Where Are You?

After I connected with Dr. David Banks, my spiritual father and mentor, he allowed me to see the King in myself and taught me that I was the solution to someone's problem.

First he helped me discover my purpose, coached me to put a demand on my potential, and trusted me to walk in my leadership role without criticizing me.

I was like that Ethiopian, reading the Bible all by myself but not getting an understanding of the plan and purpose of God for my life. It wasn't until God brought these people into my life that I began to advance. God never intended for any of us to do anything on our own. If this were true, then the children of Israel would have never cried to God for him to deliver them from the oppressive hand of Pharaoh. God heard their cry and sent Moses to bring them out of captivity and teach them the ways of God.

When the army of Israel was staring defeat in the face because they feared the Palestinian giant named Goliath, God sent a youth named David to bring the victory.

Adam, Where Are You?

It was during the time of the Judges and Israel's bondage that God sent Gideon to lead his people. God is looking for a man.

Are you willing to take your life experience and example and help some other man or child achieve success? Or will you adapt the same attitude that many others have, saying "my four and no more"?

Are you willing to lay down your life and invest in the lives of others?

I can honestly say that if it had not been for these men being obedient to the very words of Christ, I don't think I would be where I am today- using my gifts and talents for the Kingdom of God.

No matter how gifted, talented, or educated you are, having a mentor is an essential part of being successful in life. The ability to gain insight and wisdom from someone, especially one who has already accomplished what you're trying to accomplish, is priceless and holds the potential to be life-changing. It's imperative not only to have a mentor, but also to be mentored by the right person. Here are some steps that will help you search for a mentor so that you may grow.

Check their track record

Make sure whoever is speaking into your life has the experience that confirms what he saying. You can gain knowledge on your own by reading books, but you want a person who can share his life experience with you about what does and does not work.

Make sure he is accessible

A mentor should have an easily approachable personality, at least as it related to his interaction with you. This does not mean that they are available for every call or text, but it does mean that this person holds the ability to make you feel comfortable when asking questions or expressing your concerns. A mentor should be there to help. You shouldn't feel uncomfortable, or as if you have to act like someone you're not when you interact.

Find someone who listens

A mentor isn't in place to overload you with information and a laundry list of do's and don'ts. They are also there to listen. Find someone who not only wants to be heard but wants to hear what you have to say.

Find someone who believes in you

Your mentor should be undeniably excited about your future and should want you to succeed. This excitement will be an anchor for you when you begin to doubt yourself or feel as if you can't do it. The fact that they want to see you succeed will push them to encourage you to stick it out when you feel like throwing in the towel.

Remember that a mentor is a help and a guide not a guaranteed ticket to success. Success is ultimately a result of the choices you make, but a solid mentor will help you make the proper choices to see you succeed in life.

Consistently show them that you appreciate the help they are giving.

The most beautiful part of the whole exchange is that, one day, you won't only have a mentor but you'll be a mentor, as well.

Points to Ponder

- God never intended for any of us to do anything on our own.

- No matter how gifted, talented, or educated you are, having a mentor is an essential part of being successful in life.

- It's imperative not only to have a mentor but also to be mentored by the right person.

Call to action

Make a list of productive people in your life who can be mentors to you. After you have made the list, contact them and explain to them the desire you have for them to be in your life.

Make another list of individuals you have seen who need some assistance from you. When you have made the list, talk to the individuals and express to them how much you would like to help them with your area of expertise.

A Call to men

We can clearly see that society is in need of real men. When I say this please don't misinterpret me. I'm not talking about some overbearing male chauvinist who puts his foot down while he raises his voice and say's "I'm the man."

This is not the type of man I'm talking about. The man I'm speaking about is a Godly man with a Kingdom mindset who doesn't mind living his life in accordance with the principles of the Bible.

In John 6:10 is the story of Jesus feeding the multitudes. It is interesting to note whom he spoke to first. *"And Jesus said Make the men sit down(emphasis mine)."* Now there was much grass in the place. So the men sat down."

Jesus says something that is so relevant: ***"Make the Men sit down."***

Isn't it amazing that before Jesus even attempts to feed anyone he first spoke to the men? I believe with all my heart that God is calling men to sit down and really evaluate what is going on in our society. We are now in a time that we need men to step up like never before. The men are responsible for feeding the family but if the man isn't in position then families, communities, and society become handicapped. God is calling men to sit down and consider the most important things in life.

As I stated in Chapter 1, we are seeing our youth being misled, single mothers rearing the children, divorce rates increasing, gay marriage on the rise, and communities crumbling.

I can recall a conversation I had with a man about publishing this book and he encouraged me to get the message out by giving me the analogy of trying to put a coin into a machine that was out of order. The point he was trying to make is that God cannot truly deposit anything inside us until the man gets in position.

God is a God of order and He wants to feed this generation with the Bread of Life; but in order for Him to do it He first has to address the situation at hand.

Adam, Where Are You?

I want to leave you with one final example. After Isaiah had his encounter with God and He showed Isaiah exactly who He was, God then challenged him with a call to action. Isaiah 6:8 says, "Then I heard the voice of the Lord saying, "Whom shall I send? And who will go for us?" And I said, "Here am I. Send me." Isaiah answered the call. Will you stand up today and answer the call for your household, community, and family and be like the prophet and tell God to send you?

Adam, Where Are You?

Study Guide

Restoring man back to his position

80

Contents

ADAM WHERE ARE YOU?

INTRODUCTION

Adam, Where Are You?

This study guide has been uniquely prepared for personal or small group learning.

Questions have been developed to encourage group discussion and practical application of the concept in the book "Adam, Where Are You?" In light of this, it is recommended that you follow these guidelines.

1. Before starting this study guide, read the book "Adam, Where Are You?" in a relaxed atmosphere.

The study guide will help you drive home some points in the book which you might otherwise simply allow to slide by. The Study Guide is not designed to prove to you or anyone else how

Adam, Where Are You?

brilliant your answers can be. The purpose of this study guide is for your learning. That must be at the top of your priorities.

2. Have your Bible, a concordance, the book "Adam,Where AreYou?" and the Study Guide together with pen and paper. Since Satan would love to keep you from growing in God, eliminate as many distractions as possible. Concentration is essential.

3. Read each chapter before answering the questions. Look up any scriptures not written in the book. Furthermore, I would encourage you to use a concordance to check other scriptures that relate to the ones being studied. Doing this can increase your depth of knowledge and understanding.

4, Answer the questions to the best of your ability. Your personal answers can be shared with others at your discretion. Sharing with and listening to others can increase your understanding as you struggle together with the concepts in the book and in God's word.

5. The ultimate Teacher is the Holy Spirit. Open each study session with prayer, ask the Holy Spirit to illuminate your inner being. Endeavor to keep an open and unbiased mind. Do not allow any presumptions to deprive you of what the Holy Spirit might want to teach you.

My prayer is that God will enlighten your inner mind that you might better understand how to live a more meaningful life

Adam, Where Are You?

Introduction

In Genesis 3:9, God asked Adam a perplexing question "Where are you?" The very words that God spoke to Adam are still echoing in the ears of mankind after 2000 years.

Chapter 1

FOUNDATION

1. T/F Many men are afraid to pursue their relationship with God because they feel they will have to give up leisure time to develop this relationship that they see so many women involved in. They view God as an elective something that you can pick or choose whether to have or not.

2. Myles Monroe quotes in one of his books, *"A lack of understanding in the roles we play will have us continually seeing women who suffer from abuse from angry men, children who wrestle with resentment and society bearing the scars of social deterioration.* (How true is this statement)?

3. If a man builds his foundation on anything other than Christ, then he will find cracks and faults in the substructure of his life and he is living on shaky grounds. (How true is this statement)?

Chapter 2

POSITION

1. Why do you think many men avoid answering the question "Where are you in regard to your position?"

2. What is your definition of being in position?

3. Why is it important that man be in position?

4. T/F   When a man isn't in position he hinders the growth of everything he is connected to. (Explain your answer)

Chapter 3

VISION

1. How true is this statement? Finding men with real vision is a rare commodity in this 21st century. We find more men today mimicking sports figures, music artists, business men, gang leaders, and charismatic speakers than we find imitating Jesus.
   (Discuss the question)

2. What is the difference between vision and sight?

3. Has your life been viewed through the lens of vision or sight?

Chapter 4

FAMILY

1. What does this statement mean to you? "Life is a fight for territory and if you're not willing to fight for what you want then what you don't want will eventually creep in."

2. T/F Today we see so many families separating which leaves many children in this generation with tainted views on what a family truly is. This false perception has children joining themselves with gangs, clubs, and cults just to find some type of structure so they can feel secure.

3. A lack of order inside the home and family can have a young boy confessing that he is with the red or the blue. It can have young women confused about their sexuality. (Discuss)

4. T/F Most men find it hard to express their emotions. Why do most men find it hard to express their emotions?

5. Many men are interested in making a living instead of having a life. We have been giving our family so many *things* instead of giving them ourselves. (Discuss)

Chapter 5

PURPOSE

1. T/F When you don't know your purpose you will

   automatically abuse yourself.

   (Explain your answer)

2. What is purpose?

3. Define the three components of man

   - Past-

   - Potential-

   - Purpose-

4. What is your purpose according to the worksheet? (Discuss)

Chapter 6

ROLE

1. T/F (Explain your answer) Men are facing difficult times in the 21st century. Many men are confused with the direction our society has taken.

2. How do we define true manhood in a society that at times exalts women and puts men down?

3. Define:
   - *Fruitful-*
   - *Multiply-*
   - *Replenish-*
   - *Subdue-*

4. How is the biblical definition of "fruitful" different from what most men have been taught about this verse? (Explain)

Chapter 7

MENTORING

1. Why is it important to have a mentor?

2. In Acts chapter 8 verses 30-31, what was the problem with the Ethiopian who was reading the Bible?

3. What are some steps you can take in searching for a mentor?

4. Make a list of productive people in your life Who can be a mentor to you.

Adam, Where Are You?

A call to men

We can see clearly that society is in need of real men. When I say this, please don't misinterpret me. I'm not talking about some overbearing male chauvinist who puts his foot down while he raises his voice and says, "I'm the head".

This is not the type of man I'm talking about. The man I'm speaking about is a godly man with a Kingdom mindset who doesn't mind living his life in accordance with the Bible.

1. Discuss the above paragraph.

2. Think about some activities you can get involved in so you can help it become more productive.

Adam, Where Are You?

Purchase your copy of "Adam, Where Are You?"
Today at Amazon.com

If you have been inspired by this book and would like to
find out about more resources contact us at
adamwhereareyou@yahoo.com or
www.jarroddunn.com

You can also write us at

Jarrod Dunn
206 Railroad St
Sweetwater Tn, 37874
Phone Number 423.371.4015